WOULD YOU RATHER

GAME BOOK

FOR KIDS
6-12 YEARS
OLD

GREAT NEWS!

COME UP WITH YOUR OWN HILARIOUS "WOULD YOU RATHER" JOKE, AND POSSIBLY IT WILL BE PUBLISHED IN OUR NEW BOOK!

SEND YOUR JOKES TO
COOLACTIVITYBOOKS@GMAIL.COM

WOULD YOU RATHER

BOIL EGGS OR BAKE HOT CROSS BUNS?

EAT POPCORN OR TRAIL MIX FOR A HOLIDAY DINNER?

WOULD YOU RATHER

SPEND A YEAR
WITHOUT
CHOCOLATE OR
WITHOUT SODA?

DYE CARROTS OR
POTATOES
INSTEAD OF EGGS
ON EASTER?

WOULD YOU RATHER

SPEND A HOLIDAY IN DISNEY WORLD OR TAKE A HELICOPTER FLIGHT OVER THE GRAND CANYON?

GO ON A TREASURE HUNT OR AN EASTER EGG HUNT?

WOULD YOU RATHER

HAVE A LITTLE DINOSAUR OR A LITTLE UNICORN AS A PET?

CELEBRATE YOUR BIRTHDAY IN A TREEHOUSE OR IN A GIANT GINGERBREAD HOUSE?

WOULD YOU RATHER

OWN A FIRE
ENGINE OR A
DUMP TRUCK?

BE AN ASTRONAUT
OR A FAMOUS
ACTOR?

WOULD YOU RATHER

TRAVEL TO THE MOON OR TO MARS?

BE A DOCTOR OR A PROFESSIONAL ATHLETE?

WOULD YOU RATHER

BE A VETERINARIAN OR A FOREIGN LANGUAGE TEACHER?

EAT PICKLES OR SALTY CRACKERS ON YOUR BIRTHDAY?

WOULD YOU RATHER

ROAST MARSHMALLOWS WHEN IT'S SNOWING OR WHEN IT'S RAINING?

TURN INTO A SNAIL OR A TURTLE?

WOULD YOU RATHER

TURN INTO A GIRAFFE OR AN ANTELOPE?

LIVE ON AN UNINHABITED ISLAND OR IN AN UNDERGROUND HOUSE?

WOULD YOU RATHER

SEE VICTORIA FALLS, THE WORLD'S LARGEST WATERFALL, OR ANGEL FALLS, THE WORLD'S TALLEST WATERFALL?

CLIMB THE WORLD'S HIGHEST MOUNTAIN OR THE WORLD'S HIGHEST VOLCANO?

WOULD YOU RATHER

USE ONLY YOUR LEFT
HAND AT HOME OR
USE ONLY YOUR LEFT
HAND AT SCHOOL?

HAVE RABBIT
TEETH OR DOLPHIN
TEETH?

WOULD YOU RATHER

HAVE A FOX'S OR
A LEMUR'S TAIL?

BE AS STRONG AS
A RHINO OR AS
FAST AS A
CHEETAH?

WOULD YOU RATHER

HAVE COW HORNS OR MOOSE ANTLERS?

TURN INTO A BAT OR A WOLF ON FRIDAYS?

WOULD YOU RATHER

WASH DISHES OR CLEAN WINDOWS FROM SUNRISE TO SUNSET?

MAKE FRIENDS WITH A MERMAID OR A UNICORN?

WOULD YOU RATHER

EAT SPAGHETTI USING SCISSORS OR WITH YOUR HANDS?

GROW A HUGE PINEAPPLE OR A TINY CACTUS ON YOUR HEAD?

WOULD YOU RATHER

HAVE ICE CUBES
IN YOUR CEREAL
OR YOUR PASTA?

LIVE IN A CAVE
OR A METRO
STATION?

WOULD YOU RATHER

SWIM WITH A PENGUIN OR WITH A MONK SEAL?

INVENT THE FIRST AIRPLANE OR THE FIRST CELL PHONE?

WOULD YOU RATHER

SPEND A LONELY
NIGHT IN THE JUNGLE
OR ON A FLOAT IN
THE OCEAN?

HAVE A BIRTHDAY
CAKE WITH ONION
OR GARLIC?

WOULD YOU RATHER

DRINK A CUP OF LEMON OR PARSLEY JUICE?

DO A CARTWHEEL ON TOP OF A REFRIGERATOR TRUCK OR A SMALL BOAT?

WOULD YOU RATHER

PLAY FOOTBALL
OR BASKETBALL
WHILE
SLEEPWALKING?

PAT A BABY
TIGER OR A BABY
LION?

WOULD YOU RATHER

PLAY HIDE-AND-BITE OR HIDE-AND-SLEEP?

SKI ON SAND OR GRASS?

WOULD YOU RATHER

MAKE AN OCTOPUS OR A SEA URCHIN SHAPED BOAT?

HAVE A FLYING HOUSE OR A FLYING CARPET?

WOULD YOU RATHER

HAVE A MAGIC STICK OR A MAGIC BALL?

RUN AS FAST AS A HORSE OR SWIM AS FAST AS A WHALE?

WOULD YOU RATHER

BE A PROFESSIONAL PHOTOGRAPHER OR A WEBSITE DEVELOPER?

DANCE ON ICE OR HOT SAND BAREFOOT?

WOULD YOU RATHER

WIN THE LOTTERY OR SAVE A RARE ANIMAL?

QUICKLY MEMORIZE MANY POEMS OR BECOME A POETRY WRITER YOURSELF?

WOULD YOU RATHER

SPEAK TWENTY LANGUAGES OR UNDERSTAND ANIMALS?

HAVE A HAMSTER OR A GOLDFISH AS A PET?

WOULD YOU RATHER

WATCH THE BEST MOVIES BEFORE THEIR OFFICIAL RELEASE OR GET AN OSCAR FOR YOUR FILM?

LIVE IN THE WORLD WITHOUT CANDIES OR WITHOUT COOKIES?

WOULD YOU RATHER

NEVER USE THE PHONE IN THE MORNING OR BEFORE GOING TO BED?

KNIT A SWEATER FOR A POLAR BEAR OR A SCARF FOR A GIRAFFE?

WOULD YOU RATHER

HOP AS FAR AS A KANGAROO OR HAVE A KANGAROO POUCH ON YOUR BELLY?

HAVE A TINY OR A HUGE DRONE?

WOULD YOU RATHER

BE ONLY ABLE TO SLEEP IN THE ATTIC OR THE BASEMENT?

HAVE TWO ROWS OF TEETH OR LOSE HALF OF YOUR TEETH?

WOULD YOU RATHER

HAVE AN EXTRA HAND OR A THIRD EYE ON THE BACK OF YOUR NECK?

PARTICIPATE IN THE SUPER BOWL OR THE FINAL FOUR?

WOULD YOU RATHER

CONTROL THE WEATHER WHERE YOU LIVE OR PREDICT THE WEATHER AT ANY PLACE AT ANY TIME?

FIND A PLANT THAT TELLS JOKES OR AN ANIMAL THAT SINGS FUNNY SONGS?

WOULD YOU RATHER

GO ON A LONG
CAR TRIP OR
HAVE A FAMILY
GAME NIGHT?

HAVE TO WALK INTO YOUR
CLASSROOM ON HANDS OR
HOP LIKE A RABBIT FOR AN
HOUR AT SCHOOL?

WOULD YOU RATHER

FEEL VERY HUNGRY EVEN WHEN YOU ARE FULL OR BE UNABLE TO SLEEP AT NIGHT?

HAVE TO READ ONE NEW BOOK A DAY OR LEARN 100 FOREIGN WORDS EVERY DAY?

WOULD YOU RATHER

GROW APPLES THAT TASTE LIKE ORANGES OR ORANGES THAT TASTE LIKE APPLES?

BE ABLE TO DOWNLOAD NEW SKILLS FROM THE INTERNET TO YOUR BRAIN OR PLAY YOUTUBE VIDEOS IN YOUR HEAD?

WOULD YOU RATHER

SEE A ROARING
WATERFALL OR
AN ERUPTING
VOLCANO?

SURPRISE OR
MAKE PEOPLE
LAUGH ALL THE
TIME?

WOULD YOU RATHER

ONLY BE ABLE TO DRINK FROM PAPER CUPS OR EAT FROM PAPER PLATES?

EAT PLENTY OF GARLIC OR ONIONS BEFORE GOING TO THE DENTIST?

WOULD YOU RATHER

HAVE A BERRY SMOOTHIE WITH MUSTARD OR HOT PEPPER?

SNEEZE OR LAUGH UNCONTROLLABLY FOR A MINUTE EVERY TIME YOU HEAR SOMEONE LYING?

WOULD YOU RATHER

BE RAISED BY
HORSES OR
MONKEYS?

HAVE FOUR SISTERS
AND TWO BROTHERS
OR FOUR BROTHERS
AND TWO SISTERS?

WOULD YOU RATHER

BE ABLE TO IMITATE THE VOICES OF FAMOUS PEOPLE OR YOUR RELATIVES?

HAVE A SPANISH OR IRISH ACCENT?

WOULD YOU RATHER

TAKE A TAXI RIDE OR AN AIRPLANE FLIGHT UPSIDE DOWN?

MEET A BEAR OR A RHINO NEXT TO YOUR HOUSE?

WOULD YOU RATHER

BECOME AN ENGLISH TEACHER IN CHINA OR BRAZIL?

LIVE IN A HOUSE WITH CHICKEN LEGS OR WITH DRAGON WINGS?

WOULD YOU RATHER

MAKE FRIENDS
WITH A TALKING
UMBRELLA OR WITH
A TALKING SHOE?

WEAR A SKIRT OR
TROUSERS ON
YOUR HEAD?

WOULD YOU RATHER

RUN A MILE IN A SNOWSTORM OR SANDSTORM?

GET A FREE TICKET TO A BASKETBALL OR FOOTBALL MATCH?

WOULD YOU RATHER

FIND A FRIENDLY MONSTER OR A LITTLE PUPPY UNDER YOUR BED?

BE A TAXI DRIVER OR A DISC JOCKEY?

WOULD YOU RATHER

ALWAYS DRAW ON BLACK OR BLUE PAPER?

GROW ALOE VERA PLANTS OR CACTI AT HOME?

WOULD YOU RATHER

HAVE A TIME MACHINE OR A UFO IN YOUR GARAGE?

TRAVEL BACK IN TIME TO MEET LIVING DINOSAURS OR TO DISCOVER AMERICA?

WOULD YOU RATHER

LIVE VERY HIGH IN THE MOUNTAINS OR THE FAR NORTH?

SURVIVE ON APPLE JUICE OR ORANGE JUICE FOR A DAY?

WOULD YOU RATHER

HEAR A CAR ALARM
OR A CRYING BABY
EVERY TIME A PHONE
IS RINGING NEARBY?

HEAR JET ENGINES OR
JACKHAMMERS NEXT TO
YOUR WINDOW IN THE
MIDDLE OF A NIGHT?

WOULD YOU RATHER

BE AN ANIMAL LIVING IN A ZOO OR PERFORMING IN A CIRCUS?

HAVE A DOG THAT NEVER STOPS BARKING OR A CAT THAT ALWAYS MEOWS?

WOULD YOU RATHER

SAVE PEOPLE DURING AN EARTHQUAKE OR A TORNADO?

WEAR A SUPERMAN OR BATMAN COSTUME EVERY TIME YOU GO OUT?

WOULD YOU RATHER

WEAR A MICKEY MOUSE OR HOMER SIMPSON COSTUME AT SCHOOL?

SWAP BODIES WITH A RANDOM CLASSMATE OR A RANDOM NEIGHBOR FOR A DAY?

WOULD YOU RATHER

PLAY SUPER MARIO OR MINECRAFT TODAY?

PLAY CHESS OR CHECKERS WITH YOUR FAMILY MEMBERS?

HAVE A MONOWHEEL OR HOVERBOARD BIRTHDAY PARTY?

HAVE NO TOILET PAPER OR NO TOWELS AT HOME?

WOULD YOU RATHER

USE CANDLES OR
OIL LAMPS
INSTEAD OF
ELECTRIC LIGHTS?

DANCE OR SKI
FOR AN ENTIRE
DAY TOMORROW?

WOULD YOU RATHER

GO TO SCHOOL EVEN ON WEEKENDS OR NEVER BE ABLE TO EAT ANIMAL PRODUCTS?

BUILD PAPER AIRPLANES OR MAKE ORIGAMI ANIMALS LIKE A PRO?

WOULD YOU RATHER

ALWAYS WEAR ONLY GREY OR YELLOW CLOTHES?

ALWAYS HAVE TO WEAR A DIVING MASK OR A SURGICAL MASK?

WOULD YOU RATHER

HAVE A BEST FRIEND WHO
ALWAYS COMPLAINS, OR
WHO ALWAYS EXPLAINS
THE OBVIOUS THINGS?

ACCIDENTALLY
BURN THE HAIR
ON YOUR ARM OR
A $100 BILL?

WOULD YOU RATHER

COLLECT ROCKS
OR SEASHELLS?

NEVER FEEL SAD
OR NEVER FEEL
TIRED?

VISIT AN OPERA
OR A LIBRARY
EVERY WEEK?

SPEND A NIGHT IN
A TRAFFIC JAM OR
AN HOUR STUCK IN
AN ELEVATOR?

WOULD YOU RATHER

COLLECT SOAP BARS OR BACK SCRATCHERS?

LIVE IN A ROOM WITH FIVE RANDOM FOREIGNERS OR WITH A RANDOM ANIMAL?

WOULD YOU RATHER

ALWAYS WEAR A BELL AROUND YOUR NECK OR A RING IN YOUR NOSE?

HOLD A SNAKE OR A TOAD FOR A MINUTE?

WOULD YOU RATHER

LEARN ABOUT A PANDA
FROM A SCIENCE
TEACHER OR A SCIENCE
ENCYCLOPEDIA?

BE THE FASTEST
READER OR THE
FASTEST RUNNER IN
THE ENTIRE COUNTRY?

WOULD YOU RATHER

HAVE A TIGHTROPE WALKER OR A DOG FOOD TASTER IN YOUR FAMILY?

MAKE WEATHER FORECASTS OR BASKETBALL PREDICTIONS ON TV?

WOULD YOU RATHER

SEE THE PYRAMIDS IN EGYPT OR THE EIFFEL TOWER IN FRANCE?

HAVE NO LOCK ON YOUR DOOR OR NO GLASS IN YOUR WINDOWS?

WOULD YOU RATHER

HAVE TO SHARPEN
A KNIFE OR LIGHT
A BONFIRE?

BE VERY
INATTENTIVE OR
VERY MESSY?

WOULD YOU RATHER

BE ABLE TO TURN INTO A WILD LAND ANIMAL OR A WILD AQUATIC ANIMAL?

TRY A BANANA SOUP OR A BROCCOLI ICE CREAM?

WOULD YOU RATHER

ALWAYS HAVE
CLEAN HANDS OR
CLEAN TEETH?

DRINK A GLASS OF
SALTY OR OILY
WATER?

WOULD YOU RATHER

ENJOY THE MOST
AMAZING FIREWORKS
OR RIDE A GIANT
FERRIS WHEEL?

MODEL A LIFE-SIZE
PLAY-DOH LION
OR TIGER?

WOULD YOU RATHER

PAINT YOUR ROOM ON YOUR OWN OR PAINT A GARAGE WITH A PROFESSIONAL DESIGNER?

MAKE UP IMAGINARY STORIES ABOUT MONSTERS OR ABOUT TIME TRAVELERS?

WOULD YOU RATHER

COME UP WITH A NEW JOKE EVERY TIME YOU SNEEZE OR EVERY TIME YOU COUGH?

SLEEP IN A ROOM WITH A COBRA OR A BIG SPIDER?

WOULD YOU RATHER

SING A SONG ON STAGE FOR YOUR CLASSMATES EVERY MORNING OR AFTER THE LESSONS?

FILM A 3D MOVIE OR BECOME AN ACROBAT?

WOULD YOU RATHER

HAVE A WATER BALLOON FIGHT OR A GUNFIGHT WITH FOAM DART GUNS?

BECOME A TENNIS OR BADMINTON WORLD CHAMPION?

WOULD YOU RATHER

HAVE A GIANT AQUARIUM OR AN ANT FARM AT HOME?

COLLECT LITTLE AIRPLANES OR HELICOPTERS?

WOULD YOU RATHER

TAKE A SELFIE WITH A UFO OR WITH A REAL ALIEN?

PLAY WITH THE AUTUMN LEAVES IN SPRING OR WITH SNOWBALLS IN SUMMER?

WOULD YOU RATHER

RUN AN EGG-AND-SPOON RACE OR A SHOEBOX RACE?

GET A TRANSPARENT BACKPACK OR A TRANSPARENT COAT?

WOULD YOU RATHER

WEAR SUPER BAGGY CLOTHES OR VERY TIGHT CLOTHES?

KNOW THE NAME OF EVERY FLOWER OR EVERY INSECT?

WOULD YOU RATHER

POP BUBBLE WRAP OR WHISTLE LIKE A PRO?

GET A COCKROACH-SHAPED OR A SPIDER-SHAPED BALLOON AS A GIFT?

WOULD YOU RATHER

USE A
SURFBOARD OR A
BOOGIE BOARD
EVERY DAY?

WATCH THE WORLD'S
BEST 100 MOVIES OR
VISIT THE TEN GREATEST
PLACES IN THE WORLD?

WOULD YOU RATHER

BE THE MOST BRILLIANT BOARD GAME OR FOOTBALL PLAYER IN YOUR SCHOOL?

ALWAYS SLEEP WITH A GIANT TEDDY OR IN A HAMMOCK?

WOULD YOU RATHER

HAVE VERY POWERFUL BINOCULARS OR A TELESCOPE?

HAVE YOUR OWN REAL, FULL-SIZE TRAIN OR A HOT AIR BALLOON?

WOULD YOU RATHER

HAVE A TALKING PARROT OR A CHINCHILLA AS A PET?

BUILD EPIC BLANKET FORTS OR BECOME A PROFESSIONAL JUGGLER?

WOULD YOU RATHER

RIDE A BMX BIKE
OR HAVE A
BOUNCY CASTLE?

MAKE A CARTOON
OR DRAW A
COMIC BOOK?

WOULD YOU RATHER

HAVE THE MOST BEAUTIFUL PIÑATA OR THE MOST AMAZING KITE?

MAKE A HAND-PAINTED T-SHIRT OR PANTS?

WOULD YOU RATHER

TAKE A BUBBLE BATH WITH ROSE PETALS OR COCONUT OIL?

GET A CHEST OF BUBBLE GUM OR A CHEST OF ICE POPS?

WOULD YOU RATHER

OWN A JET SKI
OR LIVE ON A
TROPICAL ISLAND?

INVENT FUNNY
WORDS OR
HILARIOUS TONGUE
TWISTERS?

CREATE A FAMILY
BOOK OR WISH
MAP?

WATCH A METEOR
SHOWER OR A
TOTAL SOLAR
ECLIPSE?

WOULD YOU RATHER

HOLD YOUR BREATH FOR
A MINUTE OR WALK AT
HOME FOR A MINUTE WITH
YOUR EYES CLOSED?

PLAY KICKBALL OR
HAVE A PILLOW
FIGHT?

WOULD YOU RATHER

ENJOY A SUNRISE BREAKFAST IN THE CORNFIELD OR THE FOREST?

CREATE YOUR OWN BLOG OR OPEN A PUPPET THEATER IN A GARAGE?

WOULD YOU RATHER

MAKE HOMEMADE
MINI PIZZAS OR
CUPCAKES?

PLAY BOTTLE
BOWLING OR
CLASSIC BOWLING?

WOULD YOU RATHER

ALWAYS SIT ON TWO CHAIRS OR EAT WITH TWO SPOONS?

CREATE AN OBSTACLE COURSE OR PAINT YOUR FACE WITH FRIENDS?

WOULD YOU RATHER

DONATE YOUR OLD TOYS TO CHARITY OR TAKE CARE OF ABANDONED DOGS?

HAVE A 5-HOUR WALK IN CENTRAL PARK IN NEW YORK CITY OR IN THE GRAND CANYON?

WOULD YOU RATHER

DO MAGIC TRICKS OR
AMAZING SCIENCE
EXPERIMENTS
AT HOME?

GO SNORKELING IN
THE OPEN OCEAN OR
HAVE A BARBEQUE
ON A SMALL BOAT?

WOULD YOU RATHER

MAKE YOURSELF A BUTTERFLY OR UNICORN FACE PAINTING?

HAVE TO FIND TEN INSECTS IN THE PARK OR TEN FLOWERS IN THE FOREST?

WOULD YOU RATHER

DO SHADOW PUPPETS OR BUILD SANDCASTLES?

TAKE A HOT CHOCOLATE BATH OR COCONUT OIL BATH?

WOULD YOU RATHER

TELL GHOST STORIES
OR ZOMBIE STORIES
IN THE DARK WITH
A FLASHLIGHT?

LIVE IN A LEGO
ROOM OR SLEEP ON
THE THIRD TIER OF A
TRIPLE BUNK BED?

WOULD YOU RATHER

BUILD AN AIRPLANE OR A ROCKET FROM A KIT?

SPEAK IN A HUMOROUS VOICE OR IMITATE ANIMAL SOUNDS?

WOULD YOU RATHER

EAT A PLUM OR
AN APRICOT
EVERY HOUR?

WEAR A SHIRT EVERY
DAY WITH SKELETONS
OR ZOMBIES PAINTED
ON IT?

WOULD YOU RATHER

USE FIVE PILLOWS OR FIVE BLANKETS AT NIGHT?

LISTEN TO AUDIO CROSSWORDS OR AUDIO COLORING BOOKS?

WOULD YOU RATHER

PLAY PACMAN OR TETRIS INSTEAD OF MODERN GAMES?

CROCHET A SCARF OR A BEANIE HAT FOR A FAMILY MEMBER?

FIND A COLLECTION OF OLD STAMPS OR COINS?

TOUCH YOUR LEFT EAR OR RIGHT EAR WITH YOUR TOE?

WOW!

JOIN OUR CLUB AND GET $10 ON YOUR PAYPAL, AND SOME COOL FREE STUFF!

PLEASE
LEAVE YOUR
REVIEW

Made in United States
North Haven, CT
19 June 2022

20422067R00064